MW00653091

WHAT WILL IT TAKE TO WAKE US UP?

◆◆◆◆◆◆◆◆◆◆◆◆◆◆
**Fools No
More!!**
◆◆◆◆◆◆◆◆◆◆◆◆◆◆

By
MOSES FARRAR
Biblical Historian & Researcher

ISBN 0-9650247-3-3

MONÄMI PUBLICATIONS
PHILADELPHIA, PENNSYLVANIA

This booklet is protected by copyright © 2004
against any portions of it being copied by
unauthorized persons without written permission from its author

MOSES FARRAR

First Printing 2004
Second Printing 2005

Printed in the United States of America

TABLE OF CONTENTS

◆

DEDICATION

Dedicated to the Establishment of Peace,
Justice, Truth, and Righteousness
in the Earth.

YE PEOPLE OF THE ANCIENTS:

"It is time to awaken

within you

the Powers that Sleep!

The "Promised Land," the "Kingdom of Heaven," the "Mountaintop Experience" are all within you.

FOREWORD

FEAR IS A NATURAL EMOTION, and probably the strongest of all. If it has a rival or an equal, it is Love. I confess that I am fearful – fearful for the future of our people of African-Asian ancestry the world over. Say what you will or may about the Holy Scriptures (the Bible, realizing full well that thousands have discarded the idea of a book several millenia old governing their lives), the fact still remains that there is a scripture for every need and situation. This is not to say that there are not other sacred writings, but it is to say that the revelations of the Most High through His prophets, in my opinion, are at least equal to, if not above, all other inspired scriptures.. We do agree, as well, that "all truth is one."

If I were to sum up my feelings from the voice of the biblical prophets in this Foreword, they would have to flow from the lament of the Prophet Jeremiah, when he said:

"For the hurt of . . . my people am I hurt; I am black; astonishment hath taken hold on me. Is there no balm in Gilead; is there no physician there? why then is not the health of . . . my people recovered? Oh that my head were waters, and mine eyes a fountain of tears, that I might weep day and night for the slain of . . . my people!" (Jer. 8:21-22; 9:1.)

Several sources reveal that the African Slave Trade in the Western Hemisphere formally began in 1517, the year the Spanish resolved to encourage immigration to Latin America by allowing each Spanish settler a quota of 12 Negro slaves. The year 2017 – just 13 years from now – will mark the 500th anniversary of Institutionalized Slavery in the West, and although the so-called Emancipation Proclamation was signed 140 years ago, we as people of the Black race globally are not free.

Just where will we be as a people 25, 35, 50 years hence?

vii

I am in pain! Will it forever be this way? The answer is "No," but it will be this way until . . .! Yes, we are sick and tired, but we are not "sick and tired of being sick and tired!" And until we are, not much will change.

Where is our national unity? Where is our national Leader? Where is our courtesy and respect toward one another, or our economic empowerment? Do we support Black businesses where possible, if the service and cost are competitive? At what level is our spirituality and our morality? and on, and on, and on. The Creator has declared, *"My people are destroyed for the lack of knowledge: because you have rejected knowledge, I will also reject you, that you shall be no priest to me: seeing thou hast forgotten the law of thy God, I will also forget thy children."* Taken from Hosea 4:6, this scripture is an undeniable fact. We have rejected Him, therefore, we are rejected of Him, and our enemies now rule over us. *THINGS WILL NOT CHANGE UNTIL WE DO!*

We need to borrow a page from the book of the ancient Black biblical Israelites, and unify. Had they not organized as one man behind their fearless Leader Moses, and followed his commands, after having spent 430 years in Egypt – and at least 210 years of that in bondage – it may have taken several more centuries before they would have been freed from their oppressors. Their freedom came without them lifting a sword or a spear, but through participatory unity. Recalling the Rosa Parks story of more recent memory, again, she and her people, under another fearless Leader, won the victory without sword or spear, guns or bombs. Let's do it again!

This booklet is published as another attempt to *"open the eyes of the spiritually and mentally blind, and to bring those who sit in spiritual and mental darkness out of the prison house."*

When we come together – not if, but when – I will see you on the mountaintop!!

Earth's crammed with heaven,
And every common bush afire with God;
But only he who sees, takes off his shoes –
The rest sit round it and pluck blackberries.

CHAPTER 1

"Thank You, Black Americans"

[*The following letter was purportedly written by an anonymous group of White folk.*]

"DEAR BLACK AMERICANS:

"After all of these years and all we have been through together, we think it's appropriate for us to show our gratitude for all you have done for us.

"We have chastised you, criticized you, punished you, and in some cases even apologized to you, but we have never formally nor publicly thanked you for your never-ending allegiance and support to our cause.

"This is our open letter of thanks. We will always be in debt to you for your labor. You built this country and were responsible for the great wealth we still enjoy today. Upon your backs, laden with the stripes we sometimes had to apply for disciplinary reasons, you carried our nation.

"We thank you for your diligence and tenacity. Even when we refused to allow you to even walk in our shadows, you followed close behind believing that someday we would come to accept you and treat you like men and women.

13

"We publicly acknowledge Black people for raising our children, attending to our sick, and preparing our meals while we were occupied with the trappings of the good life.

"Even during the times when we found pleasure in your women and enjoyment in seeing your men lynched, maimed and burned, some of you continued to watch over us and our belongings. We simply cannot thank you enough.

"Your bravery on the battlefield, despite being classified as three-fifths of a man, was and still is outstanding. We often watched in awe as you went about your prescribed chores and assignments, sometimes laboring in the hot sun for 12 hours, to assist us in realizing our dreams of wealth and good fortune.

"**Now that we control at least 90 percent of all the resources and wealth of this nation, we have Black people to thank the most.** We can only think of the sacrifices you and your families made to make all of this possible.

"You were there when it all began, and you are still with us today, **protecting us from those Black people who have the temerity to speak out against our past transgressions.**

"Thank you for continuing to bring 95 percent of what you earn to our businesses. Thanks for buying our Hilfigers, Karans, Nikes, and all of the other brands you so adore.

"Your super-rich athletes, entertainers, intellectuals and business persons (both legal and illegal) exchange most of their money for our cars, jewelry, homes and clothing. What a windfall they have provided for us!

"The less fortunate among you spend all they have

at our neighborhood stores, enabling us to open even more stores. Sure, they complain about us, but they never do anything to hurt us economically." Allow us to thank you for not bogging yourselves down with the business of doing business with your own people. We can take care of that for you.

"You just keep doing business with us. It's safer that way. Besides, everything you need, we make anyway, even Kente cloth. You just continue to dance, sing, fight, get high, go to prison, backbite, envy and distrust and hate one another.

"Have yourselves a good time, and this time we'll take care of you. It's the least we can do, considering all you've done for us. Heck, you deserve it, Black people.

"For your labor, which created our wealth, for your resisting the messages of trouble-making Blacks like Washington, Delaney, Garvey, Bethune and Truth; for fighting and dying on our battlefields, we thank you.

"And we really thank you for not reading about the many Black warriors that participated in the development of our great country. We thank you for keeping it hidden from the younger generation. Thank you for not bringing such glorious deeds to our attention.

"For allowing us to move into your neighborhoods, we will forever be grateful to you. For your unceasing desire to be near us and for hardly ever following through on your threats due to our lack of reciprocity and equity – we thank you so much.

"We also appreciate your acquiescence to our political agenda, for abdicating your own economic self sufficiency, and for working so diligently for the economic well-being of <u>our</u> people. You are real troopers.

"And, even though the 13th, 14th, and 15th Amendments were written for you, and many of your relatives died for the rights described therein, you did not resist when we changed those Black rights to civil rights and allowed virtually every other group to take advantage of them as well.

"Black people, you are something else! Your dependence upon us to do the right thing is beyond our imagination, irrespective of what we do to you and the many promises we have made and broken. But, this time we will make it right, we promise. Trust us.

"Tell you what. You don't need your own hotels. You can continue to stay in ours. You have no need for supermarkets when you can shop at ours 24 hours a day. Why should you even think of owning more banks? You have plenty now. And don't waste your energy trying to break into manufacturing. You've worked hard enough in our fields.

"Relax. Have a party. We'll sell you everything you need. And when you die, we'll even bury you at discount. How's that for gratitude?

"Finally, the best part. You went beyond the pale and turned your children over to us for their education. With what we have taught them, it's likely they will continue in a mode similar to the one you have followed for the past 45 years (since school desegregation).

"When Mr. [Willie] Lynch walked the banks of the James River in 1712 and said he would make us a slave for 300 years, little did we realize the truth in his prediction. Just 13 more years and his promise will come to fruition. But with two generations of your children having gone through our education systems,

WHAT WILL IT TAKE TO WAKE US UP? / 17

we can look forward to at least 50 more years of prosperity. Things could not be better – and it's all because of you. For all you have done, we thank you from the bottom of our hearts, Black Americans. You're the best friends any group of people could ever have!
    "Sincerely,
    "All Other Americans"

Are we and our offspring headed for an additional 500 years of spiritual, mental and economic slavery? Well, the possibility exists, because:

"If you always do what you've always done, you'll always get what you've always got!"

CHAPTER 2

Mel Gibson's "*Passion of the Christ*" a Deceptive Fallacy

> *Concerning the film, Pope John Paul II reportedly said, "It is as it was!" Our reply: "Untrue; but, like all other 'Crucifixion' films, was produced to exalt Jesus as Savior of the World!"*

"THE PASSION OF THE CHRIST," if it has not done so already, is certainly projected to break all box office records. But is this film fact or fiction? Is it really a motion picture about Yeshua ben Yosef, a Hebrew Israelite prophet? Or is it about Jesus Christ the Jew, who was created by the Greco-Roman Empire and the Roman Catholic Church?

We confess, we have not seen "*The Passion of the Christ,*" which is supposed to be a depiction of the last 12 hours of the life of Yeshua (Jesus); neither do we intend to see it. We have opted not to contribute to the fattening of Mel Gibson and Hollywood's coffers, nor to extending the life of a near-2000-year-old fallacy. The obvious question is, undoubtedly, "How can you condone or condemn the film without having seen it?" And the answer is: We feel that we have seen enough snippets on TV, read enough in the print media, and heard enough comments from those who have viewed the film for

18

us to make an intelligent assessment thereof. Our knowledge of the Bible and of biblical history also affords us an advantage.

By the time this book reaches the store shelves and is discovered by the reading public (which will be about mid-June of 2004), *"THE PASSION OF THE CHRIST"* will probably have lost much of its impact, and its memory may have somewhat faded. Nevertheless, we write, however belatedly, in order that movie-goers may insulate themselves from films of this nature which are sure to be released in the future.

The reasons for our condemnation of the movie, which are many and varied, will be spelled out in detail in this chapter as completely as time and space will allow. It is not our intent to take anything away from the beauty, glory and grandeur of the filming, technology, sound affects or special effects of the movie, for that would be impossible to accomplish. But what will be dealt with in this chapter is the lack of facts on which the production is based. We contend that the "crucifixion stories" of all of Hollywood's motion pictures, past and present, have been greatly exaggerated, and we will prove this to be so from the statements of eminent authors and also from common sense points of view.

We will offer in this chapter a 5-Point Rebuttal to *"THE PASSION,"* which we are sure will raise the eyebrows of the reader and further stimulate his or her thought processes in a way that has seldom, if ever, been done before. Let us begin.

REBUTTAL #1 – YESHUA'S (Jesus') RACE

Whenever a film or documentary is produced on the life and works of someone, it is an insult of the highest degree to portray that person as one whom he or she never was. Frederick Douglass, Nat Turner, Sojourner Truth, Dr. George

Washington Carver, Harriet Tubman, Dr. Martin Luther King Jr., and many others were all heros and heroines of the Black race. Should they be pictured as Caucasians? Would it make any difference to you if they were? Yeshua (who has become the Greco-Roman Jesus) was not a Caucasian, but of African-Asian descent, and of the Black race! Why, then, is he and his biblical progenitors always portrayed by the White media as one who has the appearance of an Edomite or a European? In the Greek Scriptures (Matt. 1:1-17), the genealogy of Yeshua (Jesus) runs from Abraham to Joseph, Yeshua's father. If, therefore, he was of the seed of Abraham, David, and a host of others, as the genealogy claims, let us then consider the region where Abraham was born, his ethnicity, and the ethnicity of the people of his country.

Abraham was born in the country of Chaldea (known also as Babylonia, the capital of which was Babylon), settled by Nimrod the mighty hunter, grandson of Ham. "The Black Hamites went into Africa, and also sent many branches into Asia," is a quote from Smith's Bible Dictionary of 1863.

Abraham was the first in Scripture to be called a Hebrew. The New Compact Dictionary defines the word *"ruddy"* as a word used to refer to a "red or fair complexion, **in contrast to the dark skin of the Hebrews."** Furthermore, Abraham was in and out of Egypt and Canaan many times. These two countries were also settled by descendants of Ham – Mizraim and Canaan. So whenever you see Yeshua (Jesus) as White in films, in books, in Christian churches, on the walls of people's homes, or anywhere else, realize that you are beholding an outright fabrication of who he really was. This is not only true of Yeshua, but of all the biblical prophets, priests and kings from Abraham right through to Yeshua and his disciples. The white-skin, thin-lip, shoulder-length-hair Jesus as created by Italian painter Michaelangelo should have no place in the hearts, minds and souls of Black folk.

CONCLUSION

Yeshua's lineage runs, in reverse order, from his father Joseph, to King David, to Judah (head of the tribe of Judah), to his father Jacob, to his grandfather Abraham. Yeshua's culture and nationality, therefore, was Hebrew-Israelite. Just consider some of the countries by which these early patriarchs were surrounded: Ethiopia (first mentioned in Scripture as early as Gen. 2:13), Egypt, Canaan (and its entire family of nations), Chaldea (Babylonia), and Assyria. These were all Black nations. The final three letters in the name of Abraham (after the change from Abram) are "h-a-m". This shows a definite Hamitic connection, as the Chaldeans, in whose country he was born, were descended from Ham; Yeshua descended from Abraham. If the ruling powers, past or present, lie about a man's race, they will also lie about almost everything else pertaining to him. This is what has been happening for over 2,000 years. WHAT WILL IT TAKE TO WAKE US UP?!

REBUTTAL #2 – JESHUA'S HEBREW NAME

When he lived, no one knew him by the name Jesus, or Jesus Christ. If he were across the street right now, and you called out, "Jesus," or "Jesus Christ," he wouldn't even respond. His Hebrew name by which he was known during his lifetime was Yeshua ben Yosef (which translates into English as "Joshua son of Joseph"). *Jesus* is from the Latin/Greek *Iesous,* and *Christ* is also derived from the same two languages. During the compilation of the New Testament (first written in Greek), <u>Yeshua</u> became <u>Jesus.</u> These facts are seldom, if ever, taught in the churches or in other religious circles, and the intent may just be to keep them from the masses. His name could not have possibly been Jesus, as there is no "J" sound in the Hebrew language.

REBUTTAL #3 – "THE JEWS KILLED JESUS"

After seeing *"THE PASSION,"* along with many of his members, a White Christian minister, according to network TV, placed a large sign on his church for all to see: "THE JEWS KILLED OUR LORD!" There were tens of thousands of 'Jews' living in Jerusalem, Judea, at the time of Yeshua's crucifixion – Edomite Jews as well as the indigenous Israelites. So what the minister and millions like him are saying is that "the Jews" (all of them?) killed Jesus." Every leader of people has those of his own race and religion who love him and who hate him. John 8:31-32 speaks of "those 'Jews' who believed on Jesus." Did they, his female devotees, the multitude that followed him, and his disciples kill him, too? The film makes it appear that all or most of the 'Jews' were involved, thereby making the 'Jews' the scapegoat.

The Sanhedrin Council, consisting of 71 members, tried Yeshua and found him guilty of sedition and blasphemy. These crimes combined were punishable by death. (Sedition is defined as, "Excitement of discontent against the government, or of resistance to lawful authority.") The Council then turned him over to the Roman authorities for execution. The Sanhedrin was made up mainly of Edomite Jews and Pharisees, with Caiaphas (an Edomite) presiding as high priest. This Council worked under the orders of the Roman government, who had control of all Judea at that time. Yes, there were certain 'Jews' in high places, along with some among the populace, who wanted Yeshua killed, but it is a distortion of the facts when the conclusion is drawn that "the Jews" killed him. The Christians' holy book, the New Testament, states in John 19:34, that "one of the soldiers pierced his side, and forthwith came out blood and water." All the soldiers who participated in the Crucifixion were Romans; thus Rome was the real executioner. Rome had two principal methods of capital punishment: the guillotine for beheading (as in the case of John the Baptizer) and the cross for crucifying. It was also the Roman authorities who killed John.

Time and space would fail us to expound on such personalities as Herod Antipas, Annas, and Pontius Pilate. All of them were either Gentiles or Edomite Jews serving in high places in the Roman government in Judæa, and who were parties to the persecution and prosecution of dissenting Israelite leaders and commoners during the time of Yeshua.

A creditable Atlas entitled FORTY CENTURIES: FROM THE PHAROAHS TO ALFRED THE GREAT, published by The Britannica Society, states: "It is our intent, to give a fresh look at the Jesus of history, and tell, among other things, how the Romans were totally responsible for his crucifixion, and not the Jews, as the N.T. account depicts."

The article continues: *"For the Romans alive about A.D. 30, the life and death of Jesus was of no significance whatsoever. In the context of Roman history, Jesus was just another rebellious troublemaker. After the revolt of Spartacus thousands of slaves had been crucified in the same way as Jesus. His death was merely one more item in the list of repressions that Rome found necessary to carry out in order to consolidate her power. And yet in the end the religion which is said to have been founded by Jesus would take over the Roman Empire itself, and eventually make its way all over the world. The consequences for the subsequent history of civilization were incalculable. The early Christian authors were obviously concerned with transferring the responsibility for the crucifixion of Jesus from the Romans to the Jews."*

[EDITOR'S NOTE: The article above is just an excerpt from a 5-page chapter entitled, *"Jesus of Nazareth, Savior God of a New Religion."* The Atlas is a 9"x12" hardback, perfect-bound gem, with photos.]

And lastly, from his book entitled THE HISTORICAL FIGURE OF JESUS, E. P. Sanders writes:

"The main sources of our knowledge of Jesus himself, the Gospels in the New Testament, are from the point of view of the historians, <u>tainted</u> by the fact that they were written by people who intended to glorify their hero."

So we see from all of the foregoing that *"THE PASSION"* fails again in its attempt to prove in a factual way that *"The Jews"* killed Jesus.

REBUTTAL #4 – YESHUA'S TORTURE, TAUNTING AND CROSS-BEARING

"THE PASSION" is bloody and violent, and is rated "R". As we have already discovered, Rome had carried out thousands of crucifixions before and after the time of Yeshua. **The question that has not been asked is this: "WHY WAS THE CRUCIFIXION OF YESHUA SO DIFFERENT FROM ALL OTHERS?"** John the Baptizer was imprisoned and beheaded on a guillotine one year before Yeshua's death, yet we have not read anywhere that John was paraded up and down the streets of Jerusalem, whipped, taunted, and bearing his guillotine before his execution.

Of the thousands executed in Rome over the centuries, were they all given the same treatment and attention as was Yeshua, prior to meeting their fate? What about the two thieves who were supposedly crucified with Yeshua? No mention is made at all of their being mocked and scourged, whipped and spat upon, jeered and berated, before their deaths. Something is radically wrong with the Crucifixion story of Yeshua! When nations, ancient and modern, set their standards for capital punishment, all convicted criminals meet their fate in the same way. If the penalty is death by hanging, then all hangings are uniformly done. The same is true of beheadings, the electric chair, the gas chamber, etc., and more especially when trial and conviction procedures have been followed.

Either Rome had all the condemned thousands dragged through the streets and treated as "THE PASSION" depicts Yeshua, or it was not so of any of them, including Yeshua. "THE PASSION" is a tool which is being used to boost Christianity and to increase its ranks. TV news reports have already revealed that many Christian ministers see the film as a vehicle to increase membership of Christian churches.

Why all the hoopla? Yeshua's crucifixion was just another one in the string of many, and of a young prophet of his day who was willing to stand up for what he believed was right and face the consequences. We must take the salvational element out of the Jesus story, and see him as one who was charged with and convicted of the crime of sedition against the Roman government and of blasphemy against God. Not once have we said that he was guilty.

REBUTTAL #5 – WAS THE CRUCIFIXION A SACRIFICE FOR THE SINS OF THE WORLD?

In an interview on CNN's Larry King Live, Mel Gibson stated the following: "The crucifixion of Jesus was for all men, for all time!" This is totally untrue!

As you read the Gospels (Matthew, Mark, Luke, and John), you will not see anywhere where Yeshua/Jesus himself ever said that he died for the sins of all mankind. This could never, never be, because the Most High God has taught from ancient times through His prophets that He is against human sacrifice, and that He alone forgives sins. It is Paul's spurious doctrine which he took to the Gentile world, that "Jesus died for your sins." Yeshua's death was strictly political, not at all salvational.

Millions of Christians the world over proclaim that Jesus is God. When you ask them, "How can someone kill God?, many of them answer, "It was God the Son, not God the Father, who died on Calvary."

Dr. John Shelby Spong, an Episcopal (Anglican) Bishop of Newark, NJ and author of 15 books, states in his book, "Why Christianity Must Change or Die": "There is no hope for the revival of worship so long as an idol lives undisturbed in the place reserved for a living God." Christianity has made Jesus such an idol. Dr. Spong further writes: "Any god who can be killed ought to be killed." In an ABC-TV interview on Good Morning America, Dr. Spong stated that "he could never serve a god who could be dragged through the streets, whipped into complete bloodiness, and then crucified by the hands of wicked men." The Greeks, Romans, and the Roman Catholic Church have done a masterful job of deceiving the world! (For a complete, indepth study on the Crucifixion and on the Messiah, read our book entitled "A NON-CHRISTIAN'S RESPONSE TO CHRISTIANITY," especially the chapters on "Did Ancient Israel's Animal Sacrificial System Prefigure the Crucifixion of Jesus?" and "The Messiah.")

The Romans really did not have to crucify Yeshua, when you consider the enormous amount of blood that he lost through extreme persecution, from what was seen in "the Gospel According to Mel Gibson." They could have just continued the violence for a few more hours, and that alone would have caused the condemned one to expire.

By the way, I did not see one Black face in the movie anywhere, as I viewed the ads, read the papers, and watched the TV, although thousands of Black African and Asian people inhabited Jerusalem in those days. Also, when one considers that the Black countries of Egypt and Ethiopia were not far from Jerusalem, it just seems as though there would have been a Black presence somewhere in Gibson's film.

As we bring to a close this chapter of our book, we hope and pray that we have provided some food for thought and awakened within you the desire to study and think for yourself. The days should be few when we are just led by the nose and continue to believe what the slavemaster has taught. "Awake, Awake, ye people of the ancients, and put on your strength!"

THE FUTURE EVALUATION OF JESUS

Charles Potter, in his book entitled *The Story of Religion,* sums up his chapter on "JESUS" in this way:

"The next great 'Life of Jesus' will forever dispose of the myth that the Man of Galilee was a god who came down to earth, a deity incarnate, bringing an absolutely new revelation to mankind.

"Jesus will be seen by men of tomorrow as a student of his national literature, possessed of its quaint superstitions and all its lore of demons and angels and seven heavens and millennium, but possessed of its treasures as well. He will be known to have made few original additions to the ethics of his countrymen, but to have been so steeped in the literature of his own godly people that he remoulded it into mosaics of sermons and explanatory parables so artistically and ethically beautiful that they will last as long as the race of men endures. Even more than that, he will be thought of, by Jew and Gentile of tomorrow, as a man who really lived the best truth he knew, who took what he had read and thought, and interpreted it to humanity by embodying it in his own life.

"He successfully demonstrated truth by incarnating righteousness. When men hereafter bow to him, it will not be in homage to a deity, but in recognition of a superior craftsman in the art of living."

CHAPTER 3

Frederick Douglass' Independence Day Address (1852):

"WHAT TO THE SLAVES IS THE FOURTH OF JULY?"

Perceiving full well the irony implicit in his delivering an address which commemorated the coming of independence to the United States, Frederick Douglass lost little time in laying bare the contradiction inherent in allowing Slavery to exist within a society professedly dedicated to individual freedom.

Fellow Citizens: Pardon me, and allow me to ask, why am I called upon to speak here today? What have I or those I represent to do with your national independence? Are the great principles of political freedom and of natural justice, embodied in that Declaration of Independence, extended to us? And am I, therefore, called upon to bring our humble offering to the national altar, and to confess the benefits, and express devout gratitude for the blessings resulting from your independence to us?

Would to God, both for your sakes and ours, that an affirmative answer could be truthfully returned to these questions. Then would my task be light, and my burden easy and delightful. For who is there so cold that a nation's sympathy could not warm him? Who so obdurate and dead to the claims of gratitude, that would not thankfully acknowledge such priceless benefits? Who so stolid and selfish that would not give his voice to swell the hallelujahs of a nation's jubilee, when the chains of servitude had been torn from his limbs? I am not that man. . . .

I am not included within the pale of this glorious anniversary! Your high independence only reveals the immeasurable distance between us. The blessings in which you this day rejoice are not enjoyed in common. The rich inheritance of justice, liberty, prosperity, and independence bequeathed by your fathers is shared by you, not by me. The sunlight that brought life and healing to you has brought stripes and death to me. This Fourth of July is *yours*, not *mine.* *You* may rejoice, *I* must mourn. To drag a man in fetters into the grand illuminated temple of liberty, and call upon him to join you in joyous anthems, were inhuman mockery and sacrilegious irony. Do you mean, citizens, to mock me, by asking me to speak today? . . .

Fellow citizens, above your national, tumultuous joy, I hear the mournful wail of millions, whose chains, heavy and grevous yesterday, are today rendered more intolerable by the jubilant shouts that reach them. If I do forget, if I do not remember those bleeding children of sorrow this day, "may my right hand forget her cunning, and may my tongue cleave to the roof of my mouth!" To forget them, to pass lightly over their wrongs, and to chime in with the popular theme, would be treason most scandalous and shocking, and would make me a reproach before God and the world. My subject, then, fellow citizens, is "**American Slavery.**" I shall see this day and its popular characteristics from the slave's point of view. Standing here, identified with the American bondman, making his wrongs mine, I do not hesitate to declare, with all my soul, that the character and conduct of this nation never looked blacker to me than on this Fourth of July. Whether we turn to the declarations of the past, or to the professions of the present, the conduct of the nation seems equally hideous and revolting. America is false to the past, false to the present, and solemnly binds herself to be false in the future Standing with God and the crushed and bleeding slave on this occasion, I will, in the name of humanity, which is outraged, in the name of liberty, which is fettered, in the name of the Constitution and the Bible, which are disregarded and trampled upon, dare to call in question and to denounce, with all the emphasis I can command, everything that serves to perpetuate Slavery – the great sin and shame of America! "I will not equivocate; I will not excuse"; I will use the severest language I can command, and yet not one word shall escape me that any man, whose judgment is not blinded by prejudice, or who is not at heart a slave-holder, shall not confess to be right and just.

But I fancy hear some of my audience say it is just in this circumstance that you and your brother Abolitionists fail to make a favorable impression on the public mind. Would you argue more and denounce less, would you persuade more and rebuke less, your cause would be much more likely to succeed. But, I submit, where all is plain there is nothing to be argued. What point in the anti-slavery creed would you have me argue? On what branch of the subject do the people of this country need light? Must I undertake to prove that the Slave is a man? That point is conceded already. Nobody doubts it. The slave-holders themselves acknowledge it in the enactment of laws for their government. They acknowledge it when they punish disobedience on the part of the slave. There are seventy-two crimes in the State of Virginia, which, if committed by a black man (no matter how ignorant he be), subject him to the punishment of death; while only two of these same crimes will subject a white man to like punish-punishment. What is this but the acknowledgment that the Slave is a moral, intellectual, and responsible being? The manhood of the Slave is conceded. It is admitted in the fact that Southern statute-books are covered with enactments, forbidding, under severe fines and penalties, the teaching of the Slave to read and write. When you can point to any such laws in reference to the beasts of the field, then I may consent to argue the manhood of the Slave. When the dogs in your streets, when the fowls of the air, when the cattle on your hills, when the fish of the sea, and the reptiles that crawl, shall be unable to distinguish the Slave from a brute, then I will argue with you that the Slave is a man!

For the present it is enough to affirm the equal manhood of the *African* race. Is it not astonishing that, while we are plowing, planting, and reaping, using all kinds of mechanical tools, erecting houses, constructing bridges, building ships, working in metals of brass, iron, copper, silver, and gold; that while we are reading, writing, and cyphering, acting as clerks, merchants, and secretaries, having among us lawyers, doctors, ministers, poets, authors, editors, orators, and teachers; that while we are engaged in all the enterprises common to other men – digging gold in California, capturing the whale in the Pacific, feeding sheep and cattle on the hillside, living, moving, acting, thinking, planning, living in families as husbands, wives and children, and above all, confessing and worshipping the *God of Creation,* and looking hopefully for life and immortality beyond the grave – we are called upon to prove that we are men?

Would you have me argue that man is entitled to liberty? That he is the rightful owner of his own body? You have already declared it. Must I argue the wrongfulness of Slavery? Is that a question for republicans? Is it settled by the rules of logic and argumentation, as a matter beset with great difficulty, involving a doubtful application of the principle of justice, hard to understand? How should I look today in the presence of Americans, dividing and subdividing a discourse, to show that men have a natural right to freedom, speaking of it relatively and positively, negatively and affirmative? To do so would be to make myself ridiculous, and to offer an insult to your understanding. There is not a man beneath the canopy of heaven who does not know that Slavery is wrong *for him.*

What! Am I to argue that it is wrong to make men brutes, to rob them of their liberty, to work them without wages, to keep them ignorant of their relations to fellow men, to beat them with sticks, to flay their flesh with the last, to load their limbs with irons, to hunt them with dogs, to sell them at auction, to sunder their families, to knock out their teeth, to burn their flesh, to starve them into obedience and submission to their masters? Must I argue that a system thus marked with blood and stained with pollution is wrong? No; I will not. I have better employment for my time and strength than such arguments would imply.

What, then, remains to be argued? Is it that Slavery is not divine; that God did not establish it; that our doctors of divinity are mistaken? That which is inhuman cannot be divine. Who can reason on such a proposition? They that can, may; I cannot. The time for such argument is past.

At a time like this, scorching irony, not convincing argument, is needed. Oh! had I the ability, and could I reach the nation's ear, I would today pour out a fiery stream of biting ridicule, blasting reproach, withering sarcasm, and stern rebuke. For it is not light that is needed, but fire; it is not the gentle shower, but thunder. We need the storm, the whirlwind, and the earthquake. The feeling of the nation must be quickened; the conscience of the nation must be roused; the propriety of the nation must be startled; the hypocrisy of the nation must be exposed; and its crimes against God and man must be denounced.

What to the American Slave is your Fourth of July? I answer, a day that reveals to him more than all other days of the year, the gross injustice and cruelty to which he is the constant victim. To him your celebration is a sham; your boasted liberty an unholy license; your sounds of rejoicing are empty and heartless; your denunciation of tyrants, brass-fronted impudence; your shouts of liberty and equality, hollow mockery; your prayers and hymns, your sermons and thanksgivings, with all your religious parade and solemnity, are to him mere bombast, fraud, deception, impiety, and hypocrisy – a thin veil to cover up crimes which would disgrace a nation of savages. There is not a nation of the earth guilty of practices more shocking and bloody than are the people of these United States at this very hour.

Go where you may, seach where you will, roam through all the monarchies and despotisms of the Old World, travel through South America, search out every abuse, and when you have found the last, lay your facts by the side of the every-day practices of this nation, and you will say with me that, for revolting barbarity and shameless hypocrisy, America reigns without a rival.

NO STRUGGLE, NO PROGRESS!
By FREDERICK DOUGLASS

"If there is no struggle, there is no progress. Those who profess to favor freedom yet deprecate agitation, are men who want crops without plowing up the ground; they want rain without thunder and lightning. They want the ocean without the awful roar of its many waters. Power concedes nothing without demand. It never did, and it never will. Find out just what any people will quietly submit to, and you have found out the exact measure of injustice and wrong which will be imposed upon them, and these will continue till they are resisted with either words or blow, or with both. The limits of tyrants are prescribed by the endurance of those whom they oppress."

CHAPTER 4

FULL TEXT OF THE WILLIE LYNCH WRITINGS

FOREWORD BY FREDERICK DOUGLASS

The following treatise, to the knowledgeable, will be the missing link that has been sought to explain how we were put into the condition that we find ourselves in today. It confirms the fact that the slave-holder tried to leave nothing to chance when it came to his property, his slaves. It demonstrates, how out of necessity, the slaveholder had to devise a system for perpetuating his cash crop, the slave, while at the same time insulating himself from retribution by his unique property.

A careful analysis of the following 'writing' will hopefully change the ignorant among our people who say "Why study slavery?" Those narrow-minded people will be shown that the condition of our people is due to a scientific and psychological blueprint for the perpetuation of the mental condition that allowed slavery to flourish. The slaveholder was keenly aware of the breeding principles of his livestock, and the following treatise demonstrates that he thoroughly used those principles on his human live-stock as well, the African Slave, and added a debilitating psychological component as well.

It was the interest and business of slaveholders to study human nature, in particular, with the view to practical results, and many of them attained astonishing proficiency in this direction. They had to deal not with earth, wood, and stone, but with men, and by every regard they had, for their own safety and prosperity, the need to know the material on which they were to work.

Conscious of the injustice and wrong they were every hour perpetuat-

ing, and knowing what they themselves would do if they were the victims of such wrongs, they were constantly looking for the first signs of the dreaded retribution. They watched, therefore, with skilled and practical eyes, and learned to read, with great accuracy, the state of mind and heart of the slave, through his stable face. Unusual sobriety, apparent abstraction, sullenness, and indifference, indeed any mood out of the common way afforded ground for suspicion and inquiry. "Let's Make A Slave" is a study of the scientific process of man-breaking and slave-making. It describes the rationale and results of the Anglo Saxon's ideas and methods of insuring the master/slave relationship.

"LET'S MAKE A SLAVE"
By WILLIE LYNCH

The Origin and Development of a Social Being Called "The Negro"

[Author's Note: The "n-word" appears often in the text of the Willie Lynch Letter, and is <u>spelled out</u> in its most derogatory form. We refuse to use the word; therefore, where it appears we will employ the use of the letter "n"; and for plural, "n's".]

LET'S MAKE A SLAVE. What do we need?

First of all, we need a black "n" man, a pregnant "n" woman and her baby "n" boy. Second, we will use the same basic principle that we use in breaking a horse, combined with some more sustaining factors. We reduce them from their natural state in nature; whereas nature provides them with the natural capacity to take care of their needs and the needs of their offspring, we break that natural string of independence from them and thereby create a dependency state so that we may be able to get from them useful production for our business and pleasure.

CARDINAL PRINCIPLES FOR MAKING A NEGRO

For fear that our future generations may not understand the principle of breaking both horses and men, we lay down the art. For, if we are to sustain our basic economy we must break both of the beasts together, the "n" and the horse.

We understand that short-range planning in economics results in periodic economic chaos, so that, to avoid turmoil in the economy, it requires us to have breadth and depth in long-range comprehensive planning, articulating both skill and sharp perception. We lay down the following principles for long-range comprehensive economic planning: Both horse and "n's" are no good to the economy in the wild or natural state.

1. Both must be broken and tied together for orderly production.
2. For orderly futures, special and particular attention must be paid to the female and the youngest offspring.
3. Both must be crossbred to produce a variety and division of labor.
4. Both must be taught to respond to a peculiar new language.
5. Psychological and physical instruction of containment must be created for both.

We hold the above five cardinals as truths to be self-evident, based upon following the discourse concerning the economics of breaking and tying the horse and the "n" together . . . all inclusive of the five principles laid down above. NOTE: Neither principle alone will suffice for good economics. All principles must be employed for the orderly good of the nation. Accordingly, both a wild horse and a wild or natural "n" is dangerous even if captured, for they will have the tendency to seek their customary freedom, and, in doing so, might kill you in your sleep. You cannot rest. They sleep while you are awake and are awake while you are sleep. They are dangerous near the family house, and it requires too much labor to watch them away from the house. Above all, you cannot get them to work in this natural state. Hence, both the horse and the "n" must be broken; that is, break them from one form of mental life to another, keep the body and take the mind. In other words, break the will to resist.

Now the breaking process is the same for the horse and the "n," only slightly varying in degrees. But as we said before, you must keep your eye focused on the female and the offspring of the horse and the "n." A brief discourse in offspring development will shed light on the key to sound economic principles. Pay little attention to the generation of original breaking, but concentrate on future generations. Therefore, if you break the female, she will break the offspring in their early years of development and, when the offspring is old enough to work, she will deliver them up to you. For her normal female protective tendencies will have been lost in the original breaking process. For example, take the case of the wild horse, a female horse and an already infant horse and compare the breaking process with two captured "n" males in their natural state, a pregnant "n" woman with her infant, offspring. Take the stud horse, break him for limited containment, completely break the female horse until she becomes very gentle whereas you or anybody can ride her in comfort. Breed the mare until you have the desired offspring. Then you can turn the stud to freedom until you need him again. Train the female horse whereby she will eat out of your hand, and she will train the infant horse to eat out of your hand also.

When it comes to breaking the uncivilized "n," use the same process, but vary the degree and step up the pressure so as to do a complete reversal of the mind. Take the meanest and most restless "n," strip him of his clothes in front of the remaining "n's", the female and the "n" infant, tar and feather him, tie each leg to a different horse faced in opposite directions, set him on fire and beat both horses to pull him apart in front of the remaining "n's". The next step is to take a bullwhip and beat the remaining "n" male to the point of death in front of the female and the infant. Don't kill him. But put the fear of God in him, for he can be useful for future breeding.

THE BREAKING PROCESS OF THE AFRICAN WOMAN

Take the female, and run a series of tests on her to see if she will submit to your desires willingly. Test her in every way, because she is the most important factor for good economics. If she shows any signs of resistance in submitting completely to your will, do not hesitate to use the bull whip on her to extract that last bit of bitch out of her. Take care not to kill her, for in doing so, you will spoil good economics. When in complete submission, she will train her offspring in the early years to submit to labor when they become of age. Understanding is the best thing.

Therefore, we shall go deeper into this area of the subject matter concerning what we have produced here in this breaking of the female "n". We have reversed the relationship. In her natural uncivilized state she would have a strong dependency on the uncivilized "n" male, and she would have a limited protective dependency toward her independent male offspring and would raise female offspring to be dependent like her. Nature had provided for this type of balance. We reversed nature by burning and pulling one uncivilized "n" apart and bull-whipping the other to the point of death – all in her presence. By her being left alone, unprotected, with male image destroyed, the ordeal caused her to move from her psychological dependent state to a frozen independent state. In this frozen psychological state of independence she will raise her male and female offspring in reversed roles. For fear of the young male's life she will psychologically train him to be mentally weak and dependent but physically strong. Because she has become psychologically independent, she will train her female offspring to be psychologically independent as well. What have you got? You've got the "n" woman out front and the "n" man behind and scared. This is a perfect situation for sound sleep and economics. Before the breaking process, we had to be alert and on guard at all times. Now we can sleep soundly, for out of frozen fear, his woman stands guard for us. He cannot get past her early infant slave-molding process. He is a good tool, now ready to be tied to the horse at a tender age. By the time a "n" boy reaches the age of sixteen, he is soundly broken-in and ready for a long life of sound and efficient work and the reproduction of a unit of good labor force.

Continually, through the breaking of uncivilized savage "n's", by throwing the "n" female savage into a frozen psychological state of dependency, by killing the protective male image, and by creating a submissive dependent mind of the "n" male slave, we have created an orbiting cycle that turns on its own axis forever, unless a phenomenon occurs and re-shifts the position of the female savages. We show what we mean by example. We breed two "n" males with two "n" females. Then we take the "n" males away from them and keep them moving and working. Say the "n" female bears a "n" female and the other bears a "n" male. Both "n" females, being without influence of the "n" male image, frozen with an independent psychology, will raise him to be mentally dependent and weak, but physically strong . . . in other words, body over mind. We will mate and breed them and continue the cycle. That is good, sound and long-range comprehensive planning..

WARNING: POSSIBLE INTERLOPING NEGATIVES

Earlier, we talked about the non-economic good of the horse and the "n" in their wild or natural state; we talked out the principle of breaking and tying them together for orderly production, furthermore, we talked about paying particular attention to the female savage and her offspring for orderly future planning; then more recently we stated that, by reversing the positions of the male and females savages we had created an orbiting cycle that turns on its own axis forever, unless phenomenon occurred and re-shifted the positions of the male and female savages.

Our experts warned us about the possibility of this phenomenon occuring, for they say that the mind has a strong drive to correct and re-correct itself over a period of time if it can touch some substantial historical base; and they advised us that the best way to deal with that phenomenon is to shave off the brute's mental history and create a multiplicity of phenomenon or illusions so that each illusion will twirl in its own orbit, something akin to floating balls on a vacuum. this creation of a multiplicity of phenomenon or illusions entails the principles of cross-breeding the "n" and the horse as we stated above, the purpose of which is to create a diversified division of labor. The result of which is severance of the points of original beginnings for each spherical illusion. Since we felt that the subject matter may get more complicated as we proceed in laying down our economic plan concerning the purpose, reason and effect of cross-breeding horses and "n", we shall lay down the following definitional terms for future generations:

1. Orbiting cycle means a thing turning in a given
   pattern.
2. Axis means upon which or around which a body turns.
3. Phenomenon means something beyond ordinary
   conception, and inspires awe and wonder.
4. Multiplicity means a great number.
5. Sphere means a globe.
6. Cross-breeding a horse means taking a horse and
   breeding it with an ass, and you get a dumb, backward
   ass, long-headed mule that is not reproductive nor
   productive by itself.
7. Cross-breeding "n's" means taking drops of good
   white blood and putting them into as many "n" women
   as possible, varying the drops by the various tone
   that you want, and then letting them breed with each
   other until cycle of color appears as you desire.

What this means is this: Put the "n's" and the horse in the
breeding, or mix some asses and some good white blood, and
what do you get? You get a multiplicity of colors of ass
backwards, unusual "n", running, tied backwards-ass, long-
headed mules, the one productive of itself, the other sterile.
(The one constant, the other dying. We keep the "n" constant, for we may replace the mule for another tool.) Both
mule and "n" tied to each other, neither knows where the
other came from and neither productive for itself, nor without
each other.

CONTROLLED LANGUAGE

Cross-breeding completed, for further severance from
their original beginning, we must completely annihilate the
mother tongue of both the "n-word" and the new mule and
institute a new language that involves the new life's work of
both. You know, language is a peculiar institution. It leads

to the heart of people. The more a foreigner knows about the language of another country the more he is able to move through all levels of that society. Therefore, if the foreigner is an enemy of the country, to the extent that he knows the body of the language, to that extent is the country vulnerable to attack or invasion of a foreign culture. For example, you take the slave: if you teach him all about your language, he will know all your secrets, and he is then no more a slave, for you can't fool him any longer; and having a fool is one of the basic ingredients of and incidents to the making the slavery system.

CHAPTER 5

THE WILLIE LYNCH LETTER OF 1712

By WILLIE LYNCH

*Willie Lynch was a white slave owner
from the West Indies, brought to America to
spread his ideas on how to keep an entire
race enslaved for centuries. This is the
beginning...*

"Gentlemen, I greet you here on the bank of the
James River in the year of our Lord one thousand seven
hundred and twelve. First, I shall thank you, the gentlemen of the Colony of Virginia, for bringing me here. I
am here to help you solve some of your problems with
slaves. Your invitation reached me on my modest
plantation in the West Indies where I have experiment-
ed with some of the newest and still the oldest methods
of controlling slaves. Ancient Rome would envy us if
my program were implemented. As our boat sailed
south on the James River, named for our illustrious
King, whose version of the Bible we cherish, I saw
enough to know that your problem is not unique. While
Rome used cords of wood as crosses for standing human bodies along its highways in great numbers, you
are here using the tree and the rope on occasion.

"I caught the whiff of a dead slave hanging from a
tree a couple of miles back. You are not only losing a

valuable stock by hangings, you are having uprisings, slaves are running away, your crops are sometimes left in the fields too long for maximum profit, you suffer occasional fires, your animals are killed. Gentlemen, you know what your problems are; I do not need to elaborate. I am not here to enumerate your problems, I am here to introduce you to a method of solving them. In my bag here, I have a foolproof method for controlling your Black slaves. I guarantee everyone of you that if installed correctly it will control the slaves for at least '300 hundred' years. My method is simple. Any member of your family or your overseer can use it.

"I have outlined a number of differences among the slaves, and I take these differences and make them bigger. **I use fear, distrust, and envy for control purposes.** These methods have worked on my modest plantation in the West Indies, and they will work throughout the South. Take this simple little list of differences, and think about them. **On the top of my list is "Age": the second is "Color" or shade. There is intelligence, size, sex, size of plantations, status of plantation, attitude of owners, whether the slaves live in the valley, on hill, east, west, north, south; have fine hair, coarse hair, or is tall or short.** Now that you have a list of differences, I shall give you an outline of action. But before that, I shall assure you that distrust is stronger than trust, and envy is stronger than adulation, respect, or admiration.

"The Black slave, after receiving this indoctrination, shall carry on and will become self-refueling and self-generating for hundreds of years, maybe thousands. Don't forget, you must pitch the old Black male against the young Black male, and the young Black male against the old Black male. You

must use the dark skin slaves against the light skin slaves, and the light skin slaves against the dark skin slaves. You must use the female against the male, and the male against the female. You must also have your white servants and overseers distrust all Blacks, but it is necessary that your slaves trust and depend on us. They must love, respect and trust only us. Gentlemen, these kits are your keys to control. use them. Have your wives and children use them. If used intensely for one year, the slaves themselves will remain perpetually distrustful. Thank you gentlemen."

CHAPTER 6

MITHRAISM: FORERUNNER OF CHRISTIANITY

(Pronounced **Mith'**-rä-ism)

Definition: MITHRAISM - an oriental mystery cult incorporating elements from Zoroastrianism, the primitive religions of Asia Minor, and Hellenism, having as its deity Mithras, the savior hero of Persian myth. It constituted a serious rival of Christianity in the Roman Empire between the second and fourth centuries A.D. After the acceptance of Christianity by the emperor Constantine in the early 4th century, Mithraism rapidly declined. (Source: Encyclopædia Britannica.)

Ancient Persia is modern-day Iran. The name-change took place in 1935.

Before the 6th century B.C., the Persians had a polytheistic religion, and Mithras, god of light, was the most important of their gods. Much transpired within this mystery cult within the next three or four centuries, which is not relevant to our focus at this particular time.

The main purpose of this chapter is to show the parallelisms between Mithraism and early and present-day Christianity. After the defeat of the Persians by Alexander the Great, the worship of Mithras spread throughout the Hellenic (Greek) world. In the 3rd and 4th centuries A.D., carried and supported by the soldiers of the Roman Empire, Mithras was the chief rival to the newly developing religion of Christianity.

Many cults arose in Greece and Rome, prior to the time of Jesus, involving myths and legends of the birth, death, and resurrection of a youth representative of the sun, life, or light. The Romans would have made a cult of Jesus if they could,

47

and they did add much of the ritual of their most popular cult, Mithraism, to Christianity. The cult was introduced to Rome about the middle of the first century, and flourished throughout the second and third centuries, becoming a serious threat and rival of Christianity in the whole Western world. Originally a Persian deity, Mithras was supposed to have been born of a virgin, the birth being witnessed by only a few shepherds. Ahura Mazda had made him the deity of truth and light, a sun-god equal in majesty to the Supreme Being himself. As Mithraism moved westward it proved a fertile ground for the addition of mystic meaning. Practically all of the symbolism of †Osiris was added to the Mithraic cultus, even to the fact that Isis became the virgin mother of Mithras.

Since Mithras was a sun-god, Sunday was automatically sacred to him – the "Lord's Day" – long before Christ. On December 25th, just after the winter solstice, there were elaborate rituals and celebrations. Bells were rung, hymns were sung, candles lit, gifts given, sacraments of bread and water administered to the initiate. Between December 25th and the spring equinox (Easter, from *Eastra,* the Latin form of *Astarte*) came the mystical forty days' search for Osiris, which later was the origin for the Christian Lent. On Black Friday (Good Friday) the taurobolium, or bull-slaying, was represented. At this festival, the sacrament often comprised blood drinking. Mithras, worn out by the battle, was symbolically represented by a stone image lain on a bier as a corpse. He was mourned for in liturgy, and placed in a sacred rock tomb called "Petra," from which he was removed after three days in a great festival of rejoicing.

To be initiated into the Mithraic mystery cult, the rituals were sometimes very painful, and included trials by fire, wa-

---

†Osiris and his wife Isis were originally of Egyptian mythology, 19th c. B.C.

ter, hunger, thirst, cold, etc. Afterward, a sacrament of bread and water was given (water was used before wine in the Christian sacrament).

With these august rituals and promise of immortality, it is easy to understand why this cult spread quickly throughout Europe. The Mithraists became Christians easily, for whereas Mithras was always mysteriously abstract, Christ was literally humanized; and in religion the concrete almost always carries more force than the abstract. **There were many points of similarity in the two religions; and where differences did appear, Christianity often absorbed the Mithraic ritual.** They had the same holy day (Sunday), similar Christmas and Easter festivals, a similar sacrament in the mass, and many instances of similarity in vocabulary and litany. Both Mithras and Christ were described variously as "the Way," "the Truth," "the Light," "the Life," "the Word," "the Son of God," "the Good Shepherd." One Mithraic hymn even begins: "Thou hast redeemed us, too, by shedding the eternal blood." The Christian litany to Jesus could easily be an allegorical litany to the sun-god, Mithras. Mithras is often represented as carrying a lamb on his shoulder, just as Jesus is. Midnight services were found in both religions. The virgin mother Isis was easily merged with the virgin mother Mary. Petra, the sacred rock of Mithraism, became Peter, the foundation of the Christian Church. (See New Testament, Matt. 16:18: "Thou art Peter, and upon this rock I will build my church.) The robe of Mithras, absorbed from the older Osiris cult, was always described as in one piece, as was the robe of Jesus at the Crucifixion.

Mithraism also taught that "the soul of man came down from heaven. It crossed the seven spheres of the planets, taking on their vices (e.g., those of Mars and Venus) and was finally caught within the body. The task of man is to liberate his divine part (the soul) from the shackles of the body and to reascend through the seven spheres to the eternal, unchanging realm of the fixed stars. This ascension to the sky was prefigured by Mithras himself, when he left the earth in the chariot of the sun god." This is equivalent to the Ascension story of Jesus in the New Testament, the account of which is recorded in Acts of the Apostles 1:9:

> "And when he [Jesus] had spoken these things, while they beheld, he was taken up; and a cloud received him out of their sight."

And from that time (ca. 33 A.D.) till now, believers in the Greek Scriptures (N.T.) have embraced the idea that Jesus is in heaven. This, too, is a part of the Egyptian, Babylonian, Mithraic, Greek, and Roman mythological systems. The Jesus Ascension story, despite its appearance in the New Testament, breaks down under critical analysis.

The existence of all of the foregoing myths have made the way easier for the spread of Christianity. It had all the beauty of ritual and liturgy of the ancient cults, but brought a new warmth unknown to the earlier religions.

How is it, anyway, that the Greeks, Romans, and other Europeans who were worshippers of idol gods for thousands of years prior to the Common Era (the A.D. period) and even well into several decades of the Common Era, are now the world authorities on God and Religion? All that they know about His existence was originally taught to them by the descendants of the Hebrews/Israelites of antiquity. The very man whom they claim as founder of their Faith – Jesus Christ – was born, lived, and died a Hebrew Israelite, and was the seed of Abraham, Isaac, Jacob, Moses, Isaiah, David, and the other prophets, priests, kings and commoners of biblical times. When Greece and Rome conquered the known world at that time, they confiscated all the wisdom of the ancient Black World – Egypt, Babylon, Ethiopia, and Assyria. They now proclaim Greece the cradle of civilization. Of course, when you rule the world, you can do anything you want to!

There are now millions of Black people throughout the world (wherever they have been dispersed through the African Slave Trade over the last 500 years) who have embraced Christianity. These brothers and sisters of Africa in the Diaspora apparently know little, if anything, about the history or origins of Christianity. The most they can say is that "Jesus died on the cross for my sins." This and other near-2000-year-old *False Statements* have become Truth in the minds, hearts and souls of millions, and the *Truth* as set forth by the Almighty and Most High God through His prophets has become to them, Lies. Our people sit in darkness day after day, week after week and year after year, and are taught that Black people are Gentiles and the eternal curse of Ham, created by God to be hewers of wood and drawers of water. To express my pain, I repeat the words of the Prophet Jeremiah:

"Oh that my head were waters, and mine eyes a fountain of tears, that I might weep day and night for the slain of the daughter of my people."

SHALL WE AS A PEOPLE CONTINUE TO CHOOSE IDOLATROUS MITHRAIC CHRISTIANITY, OR SHALL WE CHOOSE THE ALMIGHTY CREATOR, HIS COMMANDMENTS, AND THE TEACHING OF HIS HOLY PROPHETS? The Choice Is Ours!

If you the Reader feel as though this chapter on "MITHRAISM: FORERUNNER OF CHRISTIANITY" has been informative and enlightening, I implore you to pass it on to the uninformed and misinformed. You will be making a great contribution toward the establishment of wisdom and understanding to a people who have been destroyed for the lack of knowledge.

CHAPTER 7

THE WHITE JEWS' CONVERSION TO JUDAISM

BEFORE WE EMBARK UPON the subject of when and how the White European Jews converted to Judaism, let us first impart some pertinent information essential to the understanding of the topic at hand.

First off, the term "JUDAISM" is somewhat a misnomer, and some Hebrew Israelite groups frown upon its use as the name for their way of life, whereas with others it is acceptable. Likewise, the term "JEW" is rejected by many.

The first mention of the word *Hebrew* in Scripture appears in Genesis 14:13, where Abram (Abraham) is referred to as *Abram the Hebrew.* Often in the Scriptures the children of Israel (descended from Abraham, Isaac, and Jacob) are called *Hebrews.* In addition, Jacob's name was changed to *Israel;* he had 12 sons whose offspring eventually developed into the 12 tribes of Israel.

It is important that we note here that the New Compact Bible Dictionary defines the word *ruddy* as, "a red or fair complexion, in contrast to the dark skin of the Hebrews."

The word *Jew* was formed from the same root word as *Judea* – from *Judah* – one of the sons of Jacob and one of the tribes of Israel. However, *Jew* was not in use until ca. 750 years after the Exodus from Egypt (II Kings 16:6). The word *Jewish* does not appear anywhere in the O.T. Scriptures, and in only one place in the N.T. (Titus 1:14.)

Abraham the Hebrew came from Chaldea, or Babylonia (the capital city of which was Babylon). His native city was

Ur, just 33 miles from Babylon. Chaldea was settled by Nimrod, grandson of Ham (Gen. 10:6-10).

The way of life which the Almighty and Most High gave to Israel through Moses and the prophets did not have a name, and did not need a name. In biblical times "religion and life were one," as there was no separation between the spiritual and the carnal. Every deed was either in harmony with, or was in violation of, that way of life. After the death of King Solomon, when ten tribes revolted and separated from two – Judah and Benjamin – the spirit of God and His favor remained with Judah. Hence, possibly, the name *Judaism* was adopted many centuries later.

CONVERSIONS

The first recorded instance of people of different nationalities becoming a part of the Israelites is found in Exodus 12:37-38, where it is mentioned that "a mixed multitude" was also among those fleeing from slavery to freedom:

> "And the children of Israel journeyed from Rameses to Succoth, about six hundred thousand on foot that were men, beside children. And a mixed multitude went up also with them; and flocks, and herds, even very much cattle."

This "mixed multitude" is defined in the biblical column reference as "a great mixture," probably consisting of people from a host of nations who had migrated to Egypt prior to the Exodus. In the wilderness under Moses there were Cozbi the Midianite and an Israelite woman (Shelomith) who was married to an Egyptian man. Ruth from the land of Moab embraced the God of Israel, and became the great-grandmother of King David. A business transaction took place between David and Araunah the Jebusite; and serving in David's army was Uriah the Hitite, husband of Bathsheba.

Both the Jebusites and Hitites were part of the Canaanite family of nations (Gen. 10:18), descended from the biblical Ham. Moab was a kinsman of Abraham and Lot.

In the Book of Esther (8:17), when the Israelites were under Persian rule (who by this time had begun to be referred to as "Jews"), ". . . Many from among the peoples of the land became Jews; for the fear of the Jews was fallen upon them."

Origin of the White European Jews

It has been documented over and over again from several sources that the original Hebrews/Israelites/Jews of ancient times were people of the Black race. The question is often asked, "If the original Hebrews/Israelites/Jews were Black, who, then, are the White European Jews?" Answer: THE WHITE EUROPEAN JEWS ARE DE- SCENDED FROM ESAU, son of Isaac and twin brother of Jacob. They are also known as "Edomites" and "Idu- means." Esau is the father of the White Edomites who, with other ethnic groups such as the Khazars (White Eu- ropeans/Caucasians) and others, make up modern Jewry as it is known today. These White groups, that is, Esau's descendants, and the Khazars (Japhetic in origin) con- verted to Judaism over the centuries.

† Philip Schaff, D.D., LL.D., in his 1985 book, *Compre- hensive Bible Helps,* writes concerning the IDUMEANS. We quote, in part:

"The IDUMEANS are the same people as the EDOMITES. Edom was situated in the Sinaitic peninsula, southwest of Palestine, a wild and rugged tract of land, but quite fertile. Its original name was Seir, and its first inhabi-

---

† Philip Schaff, Professor of Church History in the Union Theological Seminary, New York; author of "Church History," "Creeds of Christendom," "Bible Dic- tionary"; editor of "International Illustrated Commentary," and "Schaff-Herzog Religious Encyclopædia."

tants were cave-dwellers. These were expelled by the descendants of Esau, who was also called Edom, "Red" (Gen. 25:30). The Edomites were hunters, but after becoming domiciled in Seir they built cities, engaged in trade, and had a social organization, with a king, long before the Israelites, their cousins. When the latter, on their way from Egypt to Palestine, reached the frontier of Edom, they were at first denied a passage through the land and generally treated very harshly by the people, though Moses recognized the common parentage of the two nations (Num. 20:14-17). But as soon as the Israelites became consolidated and settled they took revenge. Both Saul and David conquered Edom. The hostility continued, and when Nebuchadnezzar in B.C.E. 588 destroyed Jerusalem the Edomites were his allies and took part in the massacre and the pillage. It was at this time that the Edomites removed, leaving Seir and subsequently settling in the region south of the Dead Sea – Idumea. After the return of the Israelites from the captivity the hostility between them and the Idumeans was renewed. But JOHN HYRCANUS, B.C.E. 135-105, not only subjugated the Idumeans, but COMPELLED THEM TO ACCEPT CIRCUMCISION AND THE MOSAIC LAW. They had hitherto been Baal-worshippers; NOW THEY BECAME JEWS. In B.C.E. 47, one of their great men, Antipater, was made procurator of Judea by Cæsar, and Antipater's son was HEROD THE GREAT."

John Hyrcanus (above) was the son of Simon Maccabæus, among those of the Maccabæn family who rededicated the Second Temple in B.C. 165. The celebration of Hanukah is the result of that rededication.

Herod the Great was an Edomite, and was made king of Judea by the first Roman emperor, Augustus, reigning for 37 years. Jesus was born near the end of his reign (Matt. 2:1-18). Many of the Herod family were educated in Rome or had lived there for a long time. Thus they became a sort of middlemen between Greek-Roman civilization, Greek-Roman paganism, and Judaism, to the great injury of the indigenous Israelites (Jews).

Since the conquest of Canaan by Joshua after the death of Moses, Israel had inhabited Judea, with Jerusalem as its capitol. Josephus' writings reveal that "near the close of the B.C. era the Roman Empire invaded Judea, and thus established its own government. Among those whom they put in high places were King Herod the Great, Antipas, his son, and many other Edomites." The Black Israelites descended from Abraham, Isaac and Jacob living in Judea during those times consisted of Yeshua ben Yosef (Jesus) and his followers, and the Pharisees, Sadducees, Zealots, and Essenes. The White Jews of the times were Edomites, who, as we have pointed out, were forced to convert to Judaism by John Hyrcanus. These Edomite Jews and the Khazar Jews are inhabiting the country of Israel today, and are in many other parts of the world, as well. They are believed almost globally to be the offspring of the original Israelites of biblical times.

When the Black Israelites were scattered from Jerusalem in C.E. (A.D.) 70 through the onslaught of Titus and the Roman army, thousands were killed, and tens of thousands more fled into Africa, many eventually migrating to several West African countries. Their offspring remained there for 14 centuries and were eventually caught up in the African Slave Trade, which began in 1517. We do admit, however, that it was the White European Jews who preserved the way of life known today as Judaism while True Israel was in Exile and became absorbed into other religions such as Christianity, Islam, etc. The Hebrews/Israelites lost their religious heritage and almost became invisible after C.E. (A.D.) 70. The Almighty did not completely cast them away, for thousands have now returned to teach justice and righteousness, and to gather the lost sheep of the house of Israel.

The White Khazars of Caucasus Europe Also Converted to Judaism

The Encyclopædia Britannica describes the Khazars as "members of a confederation of Turkic-speaking tribes who in the late 6th century established a major commercial empire covering the southeastern section of modern European Russia. It is fairly certain that the Khazars were originally located in the northern Caucasus region and were part of the western Turkic empire (in Turkistan).

"The Khazars seem to have been more inclined to a sedentary way of life, building towns and fortresses, tilling the soil, and planting gardens and vineyards. Trade and the collection of tribute were major sources of income. **But the most striking characteristic of the Khazars was the apparent adoption of Judaism by the khagan and the greater part of the ruling class in about C.E. (A.D.) 740. The circumstances of the conversion remain obscure, the depth of their adoption of Judaism difficult to assess; but the fact itself is undisputed and unparalleled in central Eurasian history. A few scholars have even asserted that the Judaized Khazars were the remote ancestors of many eastern European and Russian Jews.**"

Arthur Koestler, in his book *The Thirteenth Tribe*, indicates that "the majority of Eastern European Jews are Khazar and Japhetic in origin, not Semitic. They converted to Judaism in 740 A.D. The Khazars lost the name Khazars and became known as Jews." Koestler's research from anthropology, which concurs with history, refutes the Khazar claim to the status of a 'chosen race' who made their covenant with the Lord. "They are not," Koestler concludes, "descended from the biblical tribes."

John Beaty's book entitled *The Iron Curtain Over Amer-*

ica (p.16), states: "The Khazars are apparently a mixed stock with Mongol and Turkic affinities, and have no racial ancestry in Israel at all."

In Henry Ford, Sr.'s *The International Jew* (speaking about the White Jews as we know them today), said, "They are not the Old Testament people." (See page 55 of the book).

So the conclusion of the whole matter, in brief, is that the White Jews of today are mainly made up of two major peoples – the Edomites (from Esau) and the Khazars (Japhetic in origin).

Steven Jacobs, a European Jew, adds other Caucasian groups to his list of Judaism converts beside the Edomites and Khazars, when he writes in the last chapter of his book, *The Hebrew Heritage of Black Africa,* the following: "Who are the White Jews, if the Black Man comes from the ancient Hebrews? There is considerable scholarly evidence that White Jews are largely the descendants of ancient Roman, Greek, Turkish, Armenian and other Caucasian groups, who adopted, or converted, to Judaism over the centuries. Importantly, historians agree that the word 'Semite' originally had a cultural meaning, not a racial one. Thus, it was the culture of a person which determined whether he was a Semite in earlier times, not his color or race."

The scholarship supporting these facts is overwhelming, to the extent that all doubt should be erased, and the truth of the matter magnified.

CHAPTER 8

TIMBUKTU: CITY IN MALI, WEST AFRICA

FOREWORD

TIMBUKTU lies near the southern edge of the Sahara, about 8 miles (13 kilometers) north of the Niger River. From the 1300's to the 1600's, it was one of the richest commercial cities of Africa and a center of Islamic learning.

Timbuktu began as a nomad camp in about 1100. It became prominent in the 1300's with the rule of Mansa Musa, emperor of the Mali Empire, who attracted merchants and scholars to Timbuktu from northern Africa. Goods from North Africa were exchanged in Timbuktu for products from the forests and grasslands of West Africa. Camel caravans from North Africa carried cowrie shells that were used as money, as well as salt, cloth, copper, books, dates, figs, and metalwork to Timbuktu. Arab traders also brought slaves, captured or bought in Mediterranean countries. The merchants of Timbuktu traded gold, ivory, kola nuts, and slaves – all from the south. TIMBUKTU BECAME A CENTER OF SCHOLARSHIP IN HISTORY, LAW, AND THE ISLAMIC RELIGION.

It remains an important historical city that is visited by tourists and scholars. It also continues to serve as a center for trade with the north.

TIMBUKTU is a city in the West African nation of Mali, historically important as a trading post on the trans-Saharan caravan route and as a centre of Islamic culture (c. 1400-1600). Located on the southern edge of the Sahara, the city was designated a UNESCO (United Nations Educational, Scientific and Cultural Organization) World Heritage site in 1988.

Map of Mali, West Africa

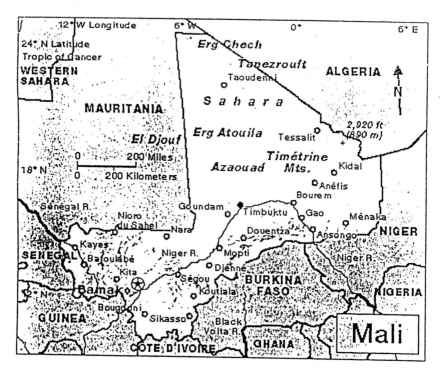

Timbuktu was founded about 1100 as a seasonal camp by Tuareg nomads. There are several stories concerning the derivation of the city's name. According to one tradition, Timbuktu was named for an old woman left to oversee the camp while the Tuareg roamed the Sahara. Her name (variously given as Tomboutou, Timbuktu, or Buctoo) meant "mother with a large navel," possibly describing an umbilical hernia or other such physical malady. Timbuktu's location at the meeting point of desert and water made it an ideal trading centre. In the late 13th or early 14th century it was incorporated into the Mali empire.

By the 14th century it was a flourishing centre for the trans-Saharan gold-salt trade, and it grew as a centre of Islamic culture. Three of West Africa's oldest mosques – Djinguereber, Sankore, and Sidi Yahia – were built there during the 14th and 15th centuries. After an extravagant pilgrimage to Mecca in 1324, the Mali emperor Mansa Musa built the Great Mosque (Djinguereber) and a royal residence, the Madugu (the former has since been rebuilt many times, and of the latter no trace remains). The Granada architect Abu Ishaq as-Sahili was then commissioned to design the Sankore mosque, around which **Sankore University** was established. The mosque still stands today, probably because of as-Sahili's directive to incorporate a wooden framework into the mud walls of the building, thus facilitating annual repairs after the rainy season.

The Tuareg regained control of the city in 1433, but they ruled from the desert. Although the Tuareg exacted sizable tributes and plundered periodically, trade and learning continued to flourish in Timbuktu. By 1450, its population increased to about 100,000. **The city's scholars, many of whom had studied in Mecca or in Egypt, numbered some 25,000.**

In 1468 the city was conquered by the Songhai ruler Sonni 'Ali. He was generally ill-disposed to the city's Muslim scholars, but his successor – the first ruler of the new Askia dynasty, Muhammad I Askia of Songhai (reigned 1493-1528) used the scholarly elite as legal and moral counselors. During the Askia period **(1493-1591) Timbuktu was at the height of its commercial and intellectual development.** Merchants from Ghudamis (Ghadames; now in Libya), Augila (now Awjidah, Libya), and numerous other cities of North Africa gathered there to buy gold and slaves in exchange for the Saharan salt of Taghaza and for North African cloth and horses.

After it was captured by Morocco in 1591, the city declined. Its scholars were ordered arrested in 1593 on suspicion of disaffection; some were killed during a resulting struggle, while others were exiled to Morocco. Perhaps worse still, the small Moroccan garrisons placed in command of the city offered inadequate protection, and Timbuktu was repeatedly attacked and conquered by the Bambara, Fulani, and Tuareg.

European explorers reached Timbuktu in the early 19th century. The ill-fated Scottish explorer Gordon Laing was the first to arrive (1826), followed by the French explorer René-Auguste Caillié in 1828. Caillié, who had studied Islam and learned Arabic, reached Timbuktu disguised as an Arab. After two weeks he departed, becoming the first explorer to return to Europe with firsthand knowledge of the city (rumors of Timbuktu's wealth had reached Europe centuries before, owing to tales of Musa's 11th century caravan to Mecca). In 1853 the German geographer Heinrich Barth reached the city during a five-year trek across Africa. He, too, survived the journey, later publishing a chronicle of his travels.

Timbuktu was captured by the French in 1894. They partly restored the city from the desolate condition in which they found it, but no connecting railway or hard-surfaced road was built. In 1960 it became part of the newly independent Republic of Mali.

Timbuktu is now an administrative centre of Mali. Small salt caravans from Taoudenni still arrive, but large-scale trans-Saharan commerce no longer exists there. Although the city has a small airport, it is most commonly reached by camel or boat. Islamic learning survives among a handful of aging scholars, and a language institute (Lycée Franco-Arabe) teaches Arabic and French. In the late 1900's, restoration efforts were undertaken to preserve the city's three great mosques, which are threatened by sand encroachment and by general decay.

The 1976 population was 19,165; in 1987, 31,962.

TIMBUKTU TIMELINE

ca. 1100 Tuareg nomads establish a seasonal camp, the future Timbuktu, at an oasis near the Niger River.

ca. 1300 Timbuktu becomes a focal point of the trans-Saharan gold/salt trade.

1325 Mansa Musa, sultan of Mali, stays at Timbuktu and builds the great Djingareyber Mosque and Madugu royal palace.

1353 Renowned Arab traveler and author Ibn Battutah visits Timbuktu and describes its splendors.

1433 Tuaregs capture Timbuktu, but they rule from the desert, and the town continues to flourish.

1468 Songhai ruler Sonni 'Ali conquers Timbuktu. During the reign of his successor, Muhammad I Askia (1493-1528), the city reaches its peak as a center of trade and Islamic learning.

1591 Moroccan troops sack Timbuktu and kill many

of its scholars. A long period of decline begins.

1828   French explorer René Caillié is the first European to visit Timbuktu and live to tell about it.

1893   The French capture Timbuktu.

1960   Timbuktu becomes part of the newly created independent Republic of Mali.

1990   Timbuktu is placed on the List of World Heritage in Danger. UNESCO establishes a conservation program to safeguard the city and its monuments against desertification.

Hebrew Israelites in West Africa Today

Hebrew villages in dusty isolated Timbuktu continue to exist despite daily hardships such as water shortages, poverty, and droughts.

Hebrew Israelites in West Africa Today

Hebrew woman of Uganda

Hebrew lad in Ghana

Hebrew Israelites in West Africa Today

Countless Israelites of African descent continue to live among native African population even to this day.

ABOVE: Abayudaya Jewess and child attend convocation in Mbale, Uganda.

BELOW: A delegation of Nigerian ews known as Ebos.

CHAPTER 9

WHAT WILL IT TAKE TO WAKE US UP?

Slave Trade & Slavery in Western Hemisphere Foretold in Scripture

IN OUR ATTEMPT TO AWAKEN the powers that sleep within the people of Hebrew-Israelite/African descent, we once again direct attention to one of the most prophetic chapters in the entire Bible, the 28th chapter of the Book of Deuteronomy.

This prophecy could not possibly apply to any other people on earth other than those who were victims of the Slave Trade and Slavery, and their descendants.

In this chapter we will simply highlight the fulfillment of this great prophecy. For a complete discussion and exegesis on Deuteronomy 28, we invite you to read Chapter 5, beginning on page 40, of our book entitled *THE DECEIVING OF THE BLACK RACE*.

Several noted authors have documented how the Black biblical Hebrews/Israelites were driven from Jerusalem in 70 C.E. (A.D.) by Titus and the Roman Army and were scattered into different parts of Africa. Among those authors are: Dr. Yosef ben Jochanan ("Dr. Ben"), Prof. Joseph Williams, Steven S. Jacobs, Prof. Rudolph Windsor, Ella Hughley, Dr. Cain Hope Felder, and Elder Moses Farrar.

Deuteronomy chapter 28 is a must-read for all peoples; it contains 68 verses. If you have not read it, we encourage you to do so. It is certain to astound you.

In the last verse of Deut. 28 (verse 68) lies the fulfillment of what has been foretold by the Almighty through His servant Moses some 3,500 years ago. As a people we have tried a plethora of ideas, suggestions and plans which we hoped would free us from this furnace of afflication in which we have been trapped for the last 500 years. None of them have worked; only the plan of the Most High will!

We know not where this message may fall; therefore, we once again throw out this lifeline for the salvation of those who are still locked in the chains of mental and spiritual bondage.

A PROPHETIC RETURN TO EGYPT

"And the LORD shall bring thee into Egypt again with ships, by the way whereof I spake unto thee, 'Thou shalt see it no more again': and there ye shall be sold to your enemies for bondmen and bondwomen, and no man shall buy you."

[AUTHOR'S NOTE: The Hebrew Holy Scriptures renders lines 3 and 4 above as, "... **And there ye shall sell yourselves** to your enemies ..."]

In Deut. 28:68 we find the prophetic statement by God that the African Hebrews would be returned to Egypt again. But, this time, "by way of ships . . . and there they would be sold unto their enemies for bondmen and bondwomen . . ." It is certain that this prophecy fell upon only one people on the face of the earth, the people of Africa – the victims of the greatest, most cruel, vicious, and horrifying slave trade in the annals of history.

In their quest to escape the onslaught of destruction that came upon Jerusalem in 70 C.E. (A.D.) by the Roman general

Titus, the African Hebrews fled westward and southward into northern and central Africa. This invasion of Jerusalem and the conquest of this region caused the final dispersion of all the remnants of the black northeast tribespeople. This flight into northern, central, and western Africa placed the African Hebrews in position for the fulfillment of the prophecy, the great African slave trade. This brought about the final phase of chastisement and the disbursement of the people of Africa into Europe and the lands of the Americas, the "New World." These African slaves were transported to the New World (a second Egypt) in the bottoms of slave ships, under the most inhumane conditions. These people were stretched out face-to-face in two lines, and in the space between their feet were others lying on their backs. The ships were packed to the brim. On board, the most frequent sicknesses were scurvy, dysentery, and the "pian," a skin disease. The high mortality rate led to a large number of suicides. Floors of the compartments were covered with so much mucous from the dysentery cases that the scene resembled a slaughter house.

God's prophecy upon Israel to "bring thee into Egypt again with ships" was fulfilled. Over 100 million people were either taken as captives or killed in the slave wars. About one-third of the Africans taken from their homes died on the way to the coast and at the embarkation stations, and another third died at sea, so that only one third survived to become the laborers in the New World.

The great captivity in the Americas not only enslaved the Hebrews of Africa physically, but it also served as a means used to remove all former knowledge, history, language, and culture from the minds of the slaves. A great international religious conspiracy was formulated to destroy the truth of their relationship with the true and living God.

The African Hebrew people have been the most abused, exploited, and oppressed peoples in all of history, and only

THE ALMIGHTY GOD can bring about their redemption and salvation. God said, *"no man shall buy you."* No man shall intercede on behalf of the African Hebrew people except that he is sent by GOD ALMIGHTY HIMSELF to break the bonds of slavery. – **Deut. 28:68.**

"WHAT WILL
IT TAKE
TO WAKE
US UP?"*!!*

BIBLIOGRAPHY

HUGHLEY, ELLA J. *The Truth About Black Biblical Hebrew-Israelites.*
Hughley Publications, POB 130261, Springfield Gardens, NY 11413.

JACOBS, STEVEN. *The Hebrew Heritage of Black Africa.* Reprinted by
permission, 1989, M. Farrar, P.O. Box 100065, Brooklyn, NY 11210.

JOSEPHUS, FLAVIUS. *The Great Roman-Jewish War:A.D. 66-70.*
The William Whiston Translation as revised by D. S. Margoliouth.
New York: Harper & Row Publishers, Inc., 1970

KOESTLER, ARTHUR. *The Thirteenth Tribe.* New York: Random
House, 1976.

POTTER, CHARLES. *The Story of Religion.* Garden City Press, Garden
City, L.I., N.Y.

SPONG, JOHN SHELBY. *Why Christianity Must Change Or Die.*
Harper San Francisco, 1998.

WILLIAMS, JOSEPH. *Hebrewisms of West Africa.* New York: The
Biblo and TannenPress, 1930

BIBLES:

The Holy Scriptures. (Masoretic Text.) Jewish Publication Society,
Philadelphia, PA
The Holy Bible, King James version.

BIBLE DICTIONARIES:

Smith's Bible Dictionary. 1863 and 1986 editions. A. J. Holman
Company, Philadelphia, PA

ABOUT THE AUTHOR

MOSES FARRAR was born in Richmond, Virginia, and is the youngest of eight children. At age seven he went to live in the Hampton Roads Virginia area, 90 miles southeast of Richmond. Shortly after his arrival there he was selected from among many others in his age group to be trained in printing, where he learned to set type by hand – one letter at a time. In the "old days" a beginner was called a "printer's devil." In 1941 his mother took him to Philadelphia to live. When old enough to enter high school he chose to attend Dobbins Vocational Technical High School, where he continued studies in printing. He has worked on the staff of several newspapers and book-making plants in Philadelphia and Virginia. In 1969 he opened his own printing business in Philadelphia, operating it for eight years.

Ordained an Elder of an international Israelite congregation in 1971 (of which he is virtually a life-long member), he has headed congregations in Atlantic City, NJ, Brooklyn, NY, New Haven, CT, Rochester, NY, and Philadelphia. After moving to Brooklyn in 1976, he again established his printing business there for 15 years.

He is considered by many to be among the leading biblicists, biblical historians and lecturers, having presented lectures and historical and spiritual seminars since 1980 at colleges and houses of worship of various religious persuasions. In 1991 Elder Farrar lectured from the stage of the world-famous Apollo Theater in Harlem, NY. The Author was chosen by the Chief Rabbi of his congregation to visit South Africa in 1991, 1992 and 1994, to assist in strengthening the spiritual work of our many associated congregations there. For 15 years he was a member of the religious panel for the training course, "Facilitating African-American Adoption," sponsored by the New York Chapter Association of Black Social Workers' Adoption Service.

Shortly after the death of his beloved wife, Naomi, in September 2004, he moved back to Philadelphia, where he now resides.

Farrar is listed in the 2000 and forward editions of *Who's Who Among African Americans*. His book titles include: *The Deceiving of the Black Race; A Non-Christian's Response To Christianity; The Hebrew Heritage of Black Africa* (co-author); *What Will It Take To Wake Us Up?; Lavinia My Mother, Naomi My Wife; Old Testament & New Testament: The Vast Differences,* and *40 Questions Often Asked Hebrew Israelites – With Answers.*

Order Author's Books By Number

Send check/m.o. payable to: "MOSES FARRAR"
Mail to: P.O. BOX 3911 • PHILADELPHIA, PA 19146
Telephone: (215) 545-0548

Book No. 1: *"The Deceiving of the Black Race"*
112 Pages – <u>$15.00.</u> (Add $3.00 S&H; total $18.00)

Book No. 2:
"A Non-Christian's Response To Christianity"
152 Pages – <u>$15.00.</u> (Add $3.00 S&H; total $18.00)

Book No. 3: *"The Hebrew Heritage of Black Africa"*
128 pages – <u>$15.00.</u> (Add $3.00 S&H; total $18.00)

Book No. 4: *"What Will It Take To Wake Us Up?"*
76 Pages – <u>$15.00.</u> (Add $3.00 S&H; total $18.00)

Book No. 5:
"Lavinia My Mother, Naomi My Wife"
[In Memory] 90 Pp., w/Plx – <u>$15.00.</u> (Add $3.00 S&H; $18.00)

**Book No. 6: *"The Hebrew Scriptures (O.T.) & The
Greek Scriptures (N.T.): The Vast Differences"***
132 Pages – <u>$15.00.</u> (Add $3.00 S&H; total $18.00)

Book No. 7:
***"40 Most FAQs (Frequently Asked Questions)
of Hebrew Israelites — with Answers"***
88 Pages – <u>$15.00.</u> (Add $3.00 S&H; total $18.00)

Book No. 8: *"Rabbi Yeshua/Jesus Not The Messiah"*
134 Pages – <u>$15.00.</u> (Add $3.00 S&H; total $18.00)

(Add.95¢ more S&H for each additional book mailed in one package)

Send me ____ copies of Book No. 1 @ $15.00 ea. Total: $_____

____ copies of Book No. 2 @ $15.00 ea. Total: $_____

____ copies of Book No. 3 @ $15.00 ea. Total: $_____

____ copies of Book No. 4 @ $15.00 ea. Total: $_____

____ copies of Book No. 5 @ $15.00 ea. Total: $_____

____ copies of Book No. 6 @ $15.00 ea. Total: $_____

____ copies of Book No. 7 @ $15.00 ea. Total: $_____

___ copies of Book # 8 @ $15.00 ea. Total: $_____

Enclosed is check/m.o. In the amount of $_____ for above books.

Name _____

Address _____

City _____ State _____ Zip _____

Telephone (_____) _____

A MESSAGE OF HOPE FROM
ZECHARIAH
A Prophet of The Almighty and Most High Elohim –

Chapter 14, Verses 1, 9 & 11 – Hebrew Holy Scriptures:

¹*"Behold, a day of YAH [the LORD] cometh . . ."*

⁹***"And YAH [the LORD] shall be King over all the earth; in that day shall YAH be One, and His name one."***

¹¹*"And men shall dwell therein, and there shall be no more utter destruction; but Yerushalayim [Jerusalem] shall dwell safely."*

HalleluYAH! HalleluYAH!

POWER CORRUPTS!

ABSOLUTE POWER CORRUPTS – ABSOLUTELY!"

*Except that one's Power is
undergirded with
A Dynamic God-consciousness!!*

Notes